I0490548

COUCH POTATO
MONEY MAKER

·······································

A Guide to Lazy Online
Earnings For Beginners

By
MICHAEL WYNNE

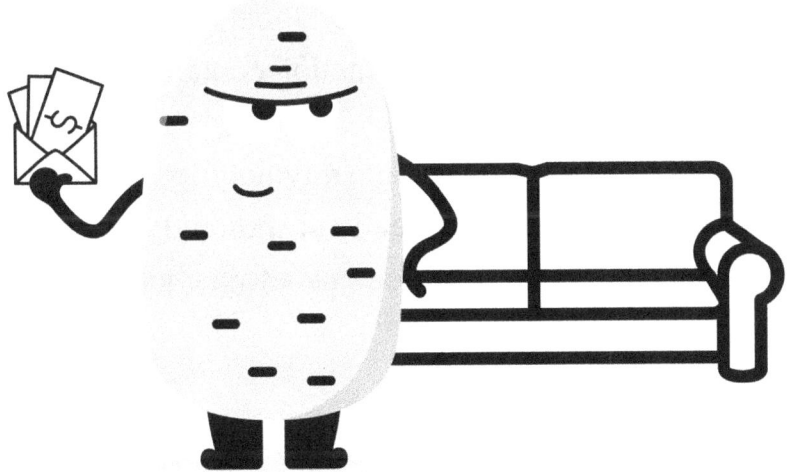

ISBN: 9798379127565
Imprint: Independently published

Affiliate Program:

If you received an electronic version of this book, there may contain affiliate links. This means I may earn commissions when you purchase products through my link at no extra cost to you.

Disclaimer:

The information provided in this book is for educational, informational, and entertainment purposes, only. The author and publisher of this book are not financial advisors or experts in any of the topics discussed. The reader should consult with a professional financial advisor before making any financial decisions.

The author and publisher do not guarantee the accuracy or completeness of any information presented in this book. The reader assumes all risks associated with using the information in this book, and the author and publisher will not be held liable for any damages or losses that may arise from the use of this information.

The reader is responsible for researching and verifying any information presented in this book before acting upon it. Any examples provided in this book are for illustrative purposes only and do not represent a guarantee of income or success.

The reader acknowledges that the tips and strategies presented in this book may not be suitable for everyone, and individual results may vary. The author and publisher are not responsible for any decisions made by the reader based on the information in this book.

By reading this book, the reader agrees to the terms of this disclaimer.

Contents

Chapter 1: Introduction   5

Chapter 2: Taking Surveys for Cash   12

Chapter 3: Passive Income with   20
Affiliate Marketing

Chapter 4: Renting Out Your Stuff   24

Chapter 5: Selling Digital Products   30

Chapter 6: Investing in Stocks and   38
Cryptocurrency

Chapter 7: Conclusion   45

Chapter 1:
Introduction

I remember the first time I made money online. I was in my early 20s, and I had just discovered the world of online freelancing.

I was able to complete writing assignments and make money from the comfort of my bedroom, and I was hooked.

Since then, I've seen the rise of the gig economy firsthand. More and more people are turning to online platforms like Upwork, Fiverr, and TaskRabbit to find work and make money.

And it's not just freelancing.

There are countless other ways to earn money online, from taking surveys to selling digital products to investing in stocks and cryptocurrency.

So, why the appeal of making money online? For starters, it offers flexibility.

You can work from anywhere, at any time, and there's no need to adhere to traditional work schedules.

This is especially attractive for those with family obligations or other commitments that prevent them from working a traditional nine-to-five job.

But it's not just about flexibility.

Making money online can also provide a sense of control over one's income.

Instead of relying on a single employer or source of income, online work allows individuals to diversify their income streams and potentially earn more money.

Of course, there are drawbacks to the gig economy and making money online. For one, the competition can be fierce.

With so many people vying for the same work opportunities, it can be difficult to stand out and secure consistent work.

Additionally, many online work opportunities are low-paying, and there's often a lack of job security or benefits.

It's important for individuals to carefully consider their options and make informed decisions before diving into the world of online work.

Overall, the rise of the gig economy and the appeal of making money online show no signs of slowing down.

As technology continues to evolve and more work becomes remote-friendly, it's likely that more and more people will turn to online work as a way to make money and take control of their careers.

Introduction to the concept of "lazy" ways to make money online

Now, let's talk about the concept of "lazy" ways to make money online.

When I say "lazy," I don't mean that you can make money without putting in any effort.

Rather, I mean that there are ways to make money online that require less time, energy, and skill compared to traditional online work opportunities.

For example, taking surveys for cash is a popular way to earn money online that doesn't require any special skills or expertise.

There are plenty of survey sites out there that pay users for their opinions on products and services.

While the pay may not be substantial, it's a relatively easy and low-effort way to make some extra cash.

Another "lazy" way to make money online is through affiliate marketing.

This involves promoting products or services on your website or social media platforms and earning a commission on any resulting sales.

While it takes some time to build up a following and establish yourself as a trusted authority in your niche, once you do, you can earn passive income without much ongoing effort.

Renting out your belongings is another way to make money online with minimal effort.

Sites like Airbnb and Turo allow you to rent out your spare room or car, respectively, for a fee.

This is a great option for those who have extra space or belongings that they're not using and want to earn some extra money without doing much work.

Selling digital products is another "lazy" way to make money online.

Creating e-books, courses, or printables requires some initial effort, but once they're created, you can earn passive income by selling them online.

I just created my first coloring book using Canva and uploading to Amazon to be sold

It had a learning curve before I finally got it submitted but even with that, I had it completed in one day.

Now it's online 24/7 with an opportunity to generate passive income.

This is a great option for those with specialized knowledge or skills that they can pack into a digital product.

Finally, investing in stocks and cryptocurrency can be a "lazy" way to make money online.

While there's always a risk involved in investing, there are plenty of resources available online to help you make informed decisions and minimize risk.

With the right strategy, investing can be a low-effort way to earn passive income over time.

Overall, there are plenty of "lazy" ways to make money online.

While they may not make you rich overnight, they can be a great option for those looking to supplement their income or earn some extra cash without putting in too much time or effort.

Chapter 2: Taking Surveys for Cash

Taking online surveys is one of the "lazy" ways to make money online that I've personally tried.

While it's not a get-rich-quick scheme, it's a low-effort way to earn some extra cash in your spare time.

When I first started taking online surveys, I wasn't expecting to make a lot of money.

However, I found that some sites paid more than others, and if I was consistent with my efforts, I could earn a decent amount of money each month.

One of the biggest benefits of taking online surveys is that it's flexible.

I could take surveys at any time, from anywhere with an internet connection.

This made it easy to fit survey-taking into my schedule, even when I was busy with other commitments.

However, not all survey sites are created equal.

Some pay more than others, and some are more reputable than others.

It's important to do your research and read reviews before signing up for any survey site.

Another thing to keep in mind is that taking surveys can be time-consuming.

Some surveys are short and only take a few minutes to complete, while others can take up to an hour.

And even after spending all that time taking a survey, there's no guarantee that you'll qualify for the full payout.

Despite these drawbacks, I found that taking online surveys was a worthwhile way to make some extra cash in my spare time.

It wasn't a huge amount of money, but it was enough to help me pay for small expenses or save up for something special.

Overall, taking online surveys is a "lazy" way to make money online that's worth considering if you're looking for a flexible and low-effort way to earn some extra cash.

While it's not a substitute for a full-time job, it can be a great way to supplement your income in your spare time.

How to find legitimate survey sites

When it comes to taking online surveys, finding legitimate survey sites is key to making sure your time and effort aren't wasted.

Here are some tips for finding reputable survey sites:

Do your research: Before signing up for any survey site, do some research to make sure it's legitimate.

Look for reviews online and check sites like the Better Business Bureau to see if there are any complaints against the company.

Look for payment proof: Legitimate survey sites should be transparent about how they pay their users.

Look for payment proof on their website or on review sites to make sure they're actually paying their users.

Check the payout threshold: Some survey sites have a high payout threshold, meaning you won't get paid until you've earned a certain amount of money.

Make sure the payout threshold is reasonable and achievable before signing up for a survey site.

Check the privacy policy: Make sure the survey site has a clear privacy policy that explains how they collect and use your information.

Legitimate survey sites should protect your personal information and not share it with third parties.

Avoid sites that require payment: Legitimate survey sites should never require you to pay a fee to join or participate.

If a site asks for payment, it's likely a scam.

Look for a variety of surveys: Legitimate survey sites should offer a variety of surveys to choose from.

If a site only offers a few surveys or they're all from the same company, it may not be legitimate.

By following these tips, you can find legitimate survey sites that will actually pay you for your time and effort.

Remember, while taking online surveys can be a "lazy" way to make money online, it's important to be smart and cautious when signing up for survey sites.

Taking online surveys can be a "lazy" way to make money online, but it's important to maximize your earnings while minimizing your effort.

Sign up for multiple survey sites: Signing up for multiple survey sites can increase your chances of qualifying for surveys and earning more money overall.

Just make sure you're not spreading yourself too thin and can keep up with the surveys on each site.

Focus on high-paying surveys: Some surveys pay more than others, so focus on the ones that offer the highest payouts for the least amount of time and effort.

You can usually tell how much a survey pays before you start, so choose wisely.

Be consistent: Consistency is key when it comes to taking online surveys.

Set aside a specific time each day or week to take surveys and stick to them.

This will help you earn more money over time and keep your survey-taking organized.

Refer friends: Some survey sites offer referral bonuses, so refer your friends to earn even more money without any additional effort on your part.

Use a survey aggregator: Survey aggregators like Swagbucks and Survey Junkie can help you find surveys from multiple sites in one place, making it easier to find high-paying surveys and earn more money overall.

Don't waste time on screeners: Some surveys start with a screener to see if you qualify.

If you don't qualify, don't waste your time on the survey. Move on to the next one and don't get discouraged.

Implementing these tips can help you increase your earnings while reducing the effort you put into taking online surveys.

Taking surveys still demands some effort and strategic thinking to ensure that your time is well-spent.

Chapter 3: Passive Income with Affiliate Marketing

Affiliate marketing is another "lazy" way to make money online, and it has the potential to earn you passive income.

In affiliate marketing, you promote other people's products or services and earn a commission for each sale that's made through your unique affiliate link.

The beauty of affiliate marketing is that once you've set up your affiliate links and promoted them, you can earn money passively as people continue to make purchases through your links.

This is honestly one of my favorite ways to earn extra cash.

It's easy to get started and once the work is done, you have passive income.

Here are some tips for earning passive income through affiliate marketing:

Choose the right products: Choose products or services that you genuinely believe in and that align with your brand or niche.

This will make it easier to promote them to your audience and make sales.

Create valuable content: Create valuable content that provides value to your audience and promotes the products or services you're affiliated with.

This can include blog posts, videos, social media posts, and more.

Build an email list: Building an email list can help you promote your affiliate links to a targeted audience who's interested in what you have to offer.

Offer a free resource or incentive to entice people to sign up for your list.

Many people think email marketing is dead but little do they know, it's a goldmine.

Use social media: Social media platforms like Instagram, Facebook, and Twitter can be powerful tools for promoting your affiliate links.

Share your content and include your affiliate links in your posts and profile.

Track your results: Use tracking software like Google Analytics or a tool like Bitly to track your clicks and conversions.

This will help you see which affiliate links are performing well and which ones may need some tweaking.

By implementing these tips, you can earn passive income through affiliate marketing and make money while you sleep.

Once you've set up your links and promoted them to your audience, you can earn money without having to actively work for it.

But once you've set up your links and promoted them to your audience, you can earn money without having to actively work for it.

When it comes to affiliate marketing, choosing the right products, creating valuable content, building an email list, using social media, and tracking your results are all essential components of a successful affiliate marketing strategy.

By following these tips and continuously improving your approach, you can earn passive income through affiliate marketing and enjoy the freedom and flexibility that comes with making money online.

With patience, persistence, and a willingness to learn and adapt, you can turn your online side hustle into a sustainable source of income and achieve the financial freedom and lifestyle you desire.

Chapter 4: Renting Out Your Stuff

We all have items lying around our homes that we don't use very often, but that others might need for a short period.

By renting out these items, we can earn money without having to do much work at all.

Here are some examples of items you can rent out:

Your car: If you're not using your car very often, you can rent it out to people who need a vehicle for a short period.

Websites like Turo and Getaround make it easy to list your car for rent and connect with potential renters.

Your home: If you have a spare room or an entire home that you're not using, you can rent it out on Airbnb or other vacation rental sites.

This is a great way to earn passive income while you're away on vacation or just living your day-to-day life.

Your parking space: If you live in a busy area with limited parking, you can rent out your parking space to people who need a place to park their cars.

Websites like SpotHero and ParkWhiz make it easy to list your parking spot and connect with potential renters.

Your camera equipment: If you're a photographer or videographer with high-quality camera equipment, you can rent it out to others who need it for a shoot.

Websites like KitSplit and ShareGrid make it easy to list your equipment and connect with potential renters.

Renting out your stuff is a great way to make money without having to actively work for it.

However, to guarantee a positive outcome for all parties involved, it's essential to take precautions and establish clear expectations for renters.

When you rent out your possessions, it's crucial to remember that you're essentially entrusting your belongings to strangers.

While most people are honest and responsible, there's always a chance that something could go wrong.

To minimize this risk, it's essential to take the necessary precautions and set clear expectations for renters.

For example, if you're renting out your car, you should make sure that the renter has a valid driver's license and is insured.

You may also want to set limits on how far the car can be driven and how many passengers are allowed.

Similarly, if you're renting out your home or a room in your home, you should establish rules about smoking, pets, and noise levels.

Setting clear expectations for renters is not only important for protecting your belongings, but it also ensures that renters have a positive experience.

By outlining your rules and expectations upfront, renters know what to expect and are less likely to violate any terms.

This reminds me of a story when I decided to rent out my camping gear to someone I found on a popular online rental platform last spring.

The renter was a young couple who were going on a camping trip for the first time, and they seemed really excited about the trip.

The day before they were due to pick up the equipment, I gave them a quick tutorial on how to set up the tent and use the stove.

I also warned them about the importance of keeping food away from the campsite to avoid attracting bears.

A few days later, I received a message from the renter thanking me for the gear and letting me know that they had a great time on their trip.

But then they added a funny story: apparently, they forgot about the food storage warning, and a bear had raided their campsite in the middle of the night!

Thankfully, nobody was hurt, and the bear only made off with a bag of chips, but the renters were understandably shaken up.

While the story is amusing in hindsight, it did teach me an important lesson.

When renting out your belongings, it's crucial to make sure that renters understand all safety instructions and precautions.

In this case, I probably should have emphasized the importance of food storage more strongly, or maybe even included a written guide with the equipment.

Overall, though, it was a positive experience, and the renters were happy with the gear and my tutorial.

Chapter 5: Selling Digital Products

Creating and selling digital products can be a lucrative way to make money online, and it's something that I've been doing for several years now.

Here are some tips and steps that I've found helpful along the way:

Choose a topic that you're knowledgeable about and passionate about.

This will make it easier to create high-quality content that people will want to buy.

Do some research and make sure that there is a market for the product that you want to create.

Look at other similar products that are currently on the market and see how you can differentiate yourself.

Decide on the format of your digital product: E-books, courses, and printables are all great options, but each requires a slightly different approach.

Create your content: This is the most time-consuming part of the process, but it's also the most important.

Make sure that your content is well-written, informative, and engaging.

Set up a sales page or website: This can be as simple or as complex as you like, but it should be easy for potential customers to find your product and purchase it.

Promote your product: Use social media, email marketing, and other strategies to get the word out about your product.

Offer special discounts or bonuses to early buyers to create a sense of urgency.

Track your results: Keep track of how many sales you're making and where your traffic is coming from.

Use this information to optimize your marketing and improve your product.

Crafting and vending digital products is a fulfilling and gratifying approach to earning money online. By adhering to these guidelines, you can develop exceptional products that your customers will adore and obtain a passive income as a result.

My experience with creating and selling my own digital products

I started creating digital products a few years ago when I realized that there was a demand for the kind of content that I was passionate about.

I had always loved writing and sharing my knowledge with others, and I saw digital products as a way to turn that passion into a source of income.

At first, I started by creating e-books on various topics related to my niche.

I spent a lot of time researching the market and finding a gap that I could fill.

I created content that I knew would be valuable to my readers and put a lot of effort into making my e-books visually appealing and easy to read.

Once I had my e-books ready, I set up a sales page and started promoting them on social media and through email marketing.

I offered special discounts to early buyers and even ran a few ads to get the word out. Over time, I expanded into creating other types of digital products like courses and printables.

Each time, I followed a similar process of researching the market, creating high-quality content, and promoting my products through various channels.

One of the biggest lessons that I learned along the way is the importance of building an email list.

Having a list of engaged subscribers has been key to my success in selling digital products.

I use email marketing to build relationships with my subscribers and offer them exclusive discounts and content.

Developing and marketing digital products has been a personally fulfilling and satisfying journey for me.

It has enabled me to impart my expertise and ardor to others while simultaneously earning a passive income.

Tips for choosing a profitable niche and creating products with minimal effort

When it comes to creating digital products, choosing a profitable niche is key.

Here are some of the top 10 categories for creating digital products in my personal opinion:

1. *Self-help and Personal Development*
2. *Business and Entrepreneurship*
3. *Health and Fitness*
4. *Finance and Investing*
5. *Relationships and Dating*
6. *Travel and Adventure*
7. *Technology and Innovation*
8. *Education and Learning*
9. *Cooking and Food*
10. *Fiction and Non-fiction Novels.*

Of course, there are many other niches to explore, so let's take a look at how to select one.

Identify a gap in the market: Look for areas in which there are few digital products available, but there is still demand.

This will ensure that your product is unique and stands out in the market.

Consider your expertise: Choose a niche that you have knowledge and expertise in.

This will make it easier for you to create high-quality content and position yourself as an authority in your field.

Research your target audience: Understand your target audience's needs, pain points, and preferences.

This will help you create products that are tailored to their needs and resonate with them.

Use templates and tools: Utilize tools and templates to make the product creation process easier and more efficient.

There are plenty of resources available online that can help you create professional-looking products with minimal effort.

Outsource when necessary: If you don't have the skills or time to create certain aspects of your product, consider outsourcing.

For example, you can hire a graphic designer to create an eye-catching cover for your e-book or hire a copywriter to help with your product descriptions.

The real key to success lies in creating products that resonate with your audience and offer unique value in the crowded digital marketplace.

With a bit of creativity and research, you can find your niche and create digital products that are both profitable and fulfilling.

Chapter 6: Investing in Stocks and Cryptocurrency

Stocks are a type of investment that represents ownership in a company.

When you buy a stock, you are essentially buying a small piece of that company.

The value of the stock can go up or down based on the performance of the company and the overall stock market.

Cryptocurrency, on the other hand, is a digital or virtual currency that uses cryptography for security.

Cryptocurrencies are decentralized, meaning they are not controlled by a central authority like a government or bank.

Bitcoin and Ethereum are two of the most well-known cryptocurrencies, but there are many others in circulation.

The value of cryptocurrencies can also fluctuate based on supply and demand and other market factors.

That's a brief oversite of what stocks and cryptocurrency are.

Now let's talk about making money through investments in stocks and cryptocurrency.

It can be a lucrative way to generate passive income but you may want to read over some tips before jumping all in.

Educate yourself: Before investing your hard-earned money in stocks or cryptocurrency, it's important to educate yourself about the markets and the potential risks involved.

Take the time to research and learn about different investment strategies, market trends, and key indicators that can impact your investments.

Choose a reliable broker: To invest in stocks or cryptocurrency, you'll need to open an account with a reputable broker.

Do your research and choose a broker with a good reputation and competitive fees.

Diversify your portfolio: One of the golden rules of investing is to diversify your portfolio to minimize risk.

Don't put all your eggs in one basket.

Invest in a variety of stocks and cryptocurrencies to spread your risk.

Stay updated on market trends: Keep up to date with the latest market trends and news to make informed investment decisions.

Read financial news and analysis, and follow experts in the field.

Have a long-term investment mindset:
Investing in stocks and cryptocurrency is a long-term game.

It's important to have a patient mindset and not get too caught up in short-term market fluctuations.

Consider dollar-cost averaging: Dollar-cost averaging is a strategy where you invest a fixed amount of money at regular intervals, regardless of the market price.

This can help you to smooth out market fluctuations and potentially reduce risk.

Investing in stocks and cryptocurrency carries risk, and there are no guarantees of profit.

I caution you when considering this as a way to generate passive income.

I have lost more than I care to talk about in this book, so please be careful.

Have a long-term investment mindset:
Investing in stocks and cryptocurrency is a long-term game.

It's important to have a patient mindset and not get too caught up in short-term market fluctuations.

Consider dollar-cost averaging: Dollar-cost averaging is a strategy where you invest a fixed amount of money at regular intervals, regardless of the market price.

This can help you to smooth out market fluctuations and potentially reduce risk.

Investing in stocks and cryptocurrency carries risk, and there are no guarantees of profit.

Here's a story about a friend of mine who has experience investing in stocks and cryptocurrency

My friend, let's call him John, has been investing in stocks and cryptocurrency for several years now.

He started with a small amount of money and has been able to grow his portfolio significantly over time.

One of John's most successful investments was in a technology company that he had been following closely for several months.

He noticed that the company was consistently reporting strong earnings and had a solid track record of growth.

So, he decided to invest a significant amount of money in the company's stock.

A few months later, the company's stock price had gone up significantly, and John was able to sell his shares for a sizable profit.

He reinvested some of that money into other stocks and cryptocurrency, diversifying his portfolio to minimize risk.

John's experience with cryptocurrency has also been positive.

He began investing in Bitcoin several years ago when it was still relatively unknown, but he believed in the technology behind it.

Over time, the value of his Bitcoin investment has increased significantly, and he has also invested in other cryptocurrencies like Ethereum and Litecoin.

John's overall experience investing in stocks and cryptocurrency has been a successful one but keep in mind, it's not the same for everyone.

Chapter 7: Conclusion

In this book, we've covered a range of "lazy" ways to make money online, from taking online surveys to renting out your stuff and creating digital products.

We've explored the rise of the gig economy and the appeal of making money from the comfort of your own home.

We've also discussed the potential for earning passive income through investments in stocks and cryptocurrency.

Throughout the book, we've shared personal experiences and provided practical tips for maximizing earnings while minimizing effort.

We've emphasized the importance of doing your research, setting clear expectations, and taking calculated risks to ensure a positive outcome.

Now, it's time to take action and start earning money online with minimal effort.

Whether you choose to take online surveys, rent out your stuff, or invest in stocks and cryptocurrency, remember that success requires effort and strategy.

But with the right mindset and approach, you can turn your "lazy" habits into a source of passive income.

So, what are you waiting for? Take the first step towards financial freedom and start exploring the many opportunities available to you online.

Who knows, you might just discover a new passion or skill along the way.

Good luck!